The Best of Mary Maxim®

Warm Up *with* Knits

LEISURE ARTS, INC. • Maumelle, Arkansas

Ribbed Collar

 EASY

SIZE INFORMATION

Finished: 12" x 32" [30.5 x 81 cm]

GAUGE INFORMATION

8 sts and 10 rows to 4" [10 cm],
measured over k1, p1 ribbing using
suggested needle or any size needle
which will give the correct gauge.

INSTRUCTIONS

Bottom Half: Cast on 58 sts.

Do not join, but work back and forth on circular needle as follows:

Row 1: K1, *p2, k1; rep from * to end.

Row 2: P1, *k2, p1; rep from * to end.

Repeat these 2 rows until piece measures 7"[18 cm] from cast on edge, ending after a Row 2 and dec one st in center of row. (57 sts)

Top Half:

Row 1: K1, * p1, k1; rep from * to end.

Row 2: P1, *k1, p1; rep from * to end.

Rep these 2 rows until piece measures 12" [30.5 cm] from cast on edge.

Cast off ribwise.

On Bottom Half, sew 3 buttons in first p2 column, spaced evenly apart.

Push buttons between sts to close.

Cable & Rib Scarf

 INTERMEDIATE

SHOPPING LIST

Yarn (Light Worsted)

Mary Maxim Milan

[3.5 ounces, 219 yards

(100 grams, 200 meters) per ball]:

☐ Any Color   1 ball

Knitting Needles

☐ Size 7 (4.50 mm)

   or size needed for gauge

Additional Supplies

☐ Cable needle

☐ ¹/₂" (12 mm) Buttons - 2

☐ Sewing needle

☐ Matching thread

SIZE INFORMATION

Finished: 4.5" x 23" [11.5 x 58.5 cm]

GAUGE INFORMATION

Cable (10 sts) = 1" [2.5 cm] wide and 13 rows to 2" [5 cm] measured over pattern using **suggested** needles or any size needles which will give the correct stitch gauge.

─ STITCH GUIDE ─

tbl   Through back of loop

C6B   Slip next 3 sts onto cable needle and hold to back of work, k3 from left needle, then k3 from cable needle.

C6F   Slip next 3 sts onto cable needle and hold to front of work, k3 from left needle, then k3 from cable needle.

INSTRUCTIONS

Cast on 29 sts.

Beginning Row 1: (right side) K1, p1, [k1 tbl, p1] twice, [inc 1 st in next st knitwise] 3 times, p1, [k1 tbl, p1] 5 times, [inc 1 st in next st knitwise] 3 times, [p1, k1 tbl] twice, p1, k1. (35 sts)

Beginning Row 2: P1, k1, [p1 tbl, k1] twice, p6, k1, [p1 tbl, k1] 5 times, p6, [k1, p1 tbl] twice, p1, k1.

Now work in pattern as follows:

Row 1: (right side) K1, p1, [k1 tbl, p1] twice, k6, [p1, k1 tbl] 5 times, p1, k6, [p1, k1 tbl] twice, p1, k1.

Row 2 and every alternate row: P1, k1, [p1 tbl, k1] twice, p6, [k1, p1 tbl] 5 times, k1, p6, [k1, p1 tbl] twice, k1, p1.

Rows 3, 7, 9 and 11: As Row 1.

Row 5: K1, p1, [k1tbl, p1] twice, C6F, [p1, k1 tbl] 5 times, p1, C6B, [p1, k1 tbl] twice, p1, k1.

Row 12: As Row 2.

Repeat these 12 rows of pattern 10 times more, then Rows 1-6 once.

Next Row: K1, p1, [k1 tbl, p1] twice, k3, yo, k3, p1, [k1 tbl, p1] 5 times, k3, yo, k3, [p1, k1 tbl] twice, p1, k1. (37 sts)

Next Row: As Row 2, but purl the yo's.

Next Row: K1, p1, [k1 tbl, p1] twice, k2tog, k3, k2tog, p1, [k1 tbl, p1] 5 times, k2tog, k3, k2tog, [p1, k1 tbl] twice, p1, k1. (33 sts)

Cast off in pattern.

Sew buttons to side of scarf to match buttonholes.

Classic Tam

SHOPPING LIST

Yarn (Bulky Weight)

Mary Maxim Classic
[3.5 ounces, 130 yards
(100 grams, 120 meters) per ball]:

☐ Any Color   1 ball

Knitting Needles

Set of Double Point Needles
☐ Size 8 (5.00 mm)
16" (40 cm) Circular Needle
☐ Size 8 (5.00 mm)
or size needed for gauge

Additional Supplies

☐ Marker

SIZE INFORMATION

Finished: 20" [51 cm] circumference

GAUGE INFORMATION

8 sts and 12 rnds to 2" [5 cm]
measured over pattern using
suggested needles or any size
needles which will give the correct
gauge.

── STITCH GUIDE ──

kfb   Knit into front and back of
next st

INSTRUCTIONS

Using circular needle, cast on 72 sts.
Join in rnd, taking care that sts are not
twisted. Place a marker after last st to
indicate end of rnds.

Now work in k1, p1 ribbing until band
measures 1" [2.5 cm].

Next Rnd: *K1, kfb; rep from * around.
(108 sts)

Now work in Lace Pattern as follows:

Rnd 1: *Yo, k2tog; rep from * around.

Rnds 2 and 3: Knit.

Rnd 4: As Rnd 1.

Rnds 5-7: Knit.

Rnd 8: As Rnd 1.

Rnds 9-12: Knit.

Rnd 13: As Rnd 1.

Rnds 14-18: Knit.

Rnd 19: As Rnd 1.

Rnd 20: Knit.

To Shape Crown:

Note: When number of sts becomes
too few to work easily, change to
double point needles.

Rnd 21: *K 10, k2tog; rep from *
around. (99 sts)

Rnd 22: *K9, k2tog; rep from * around.
(90 sts)

Rnd 23: *K8, k2tog; rep from * around.
(81 sts)

Rnd 24: *K7, k2tog; rep from * around.
(72 sts)

Rnd 25: Knit.

Rnd 26: *Yo, k2tog; rep from * around.

Rnd 27: Knit.

Rnd 28: *K6, k2tog; rep from * around.
(63 sts)

Rnd 29: *K5, k2tog; rep from * around.
(54 sts)

Rnd 30: *K4, k2tog; rep from * around.
(45 sts)

Rnd 31: *K3, k2tog; rep from * around.
(36 sts)

Rnd 32: Knit.

Rnd 33: *Yo, k2tog; rep from * around.

Rnd 34: Knit.

Rnd 35: *K2, k2tog; rep from * around.
(27 sts)

Rnd 36: *K1, k2tog; rep from * around.
(18 sts)

Rnd 37: *K2tog; rep from * around.
(9 sts)

Break yarn, leaving a 6" [15 cm] tail.
Thread tail through rem sts, pull
tightly to gather and fasten off
securely.

Weave in ends.

Arrowhead Cable Set

▮▮▮▯ INTERMEDIATE

SHOPPING LIST

Yarn (Bulky Weight)

Mary Maxim Titan

[3 ounces, 80 yards

(85 grams, 73 meters) per skein]:

☐ Brown   4 skeins

Knitting Needles

Set of 4 Double Point Needles

☐ Size 10 (6.00 mm)

    or size needed for gauge

Additional Supplies

☐ 1" (25 mm) Button

☐ Sewing needle

☐ Matching thread

☐ Markers

SIZE INFORMATION

Hat: Fits up to 24" [61 cm] circumference

Mitt Length: 14" [35.5 cm] long

GAUGE INFORMATION

10 sts and 9 rows to 2" [5 cm] measured over ribbing using **suggested** needles or any size needles which will give the correct gauge.

── STITCH GUIDE ──

ssk   Slip next 2 sts knitwise, one at a time, to right needle, then insert left needle through fronts of both sts and k2tog as usual.

T3B   Slip next st onto cable needle and hold to back of work, k2 from left needle, p1 from cable needle.

T3F   Slip next 2 sts onto cable needle and hold to front of work, p1 from left needle, k2 from cable needle.

Cable Pattern: (worked over 10 sts)
Rnds 1 and 2: P1, k8, p1.
Rnd 3: P2, T3B, T3F, p2.
Rnd 4: [P2, k2] twice, p2.
Rnd 5: P1, T3B, p2, T3F, p1.
Rnd 6: P1, k2, p4, k2, p1.
Repeat these 6 rnds for pattern.

INSTRUCTIONS
MITTENS

Right Mitten:

**Cast on 43 sts, dividing sts onto 3 needles (15;14;14).

Join in rnd, taking care that sts are not twisted.

Place a M on last st to indicate end of rnds.

Rnd 1: [K1, p1] 8 times, k1, place a M, work Rnd 1 of Cable pattern over next 10 sts, place a M,
[k1, p1] 8 times.

Rnd 2: [K1, p1] 8 times, k1, sl M, work Rnd 2 of Cable to next M, sl M,
[k1, p1] 8 times.

Now keeping ribbing correct outside M's as set and working the next correct rnd of Cable pattern, continue until 13 rnds have been completed.

Rnd 14: [K1, p1] 6 times, sl 1, k2tog, psso, p1, k1, sl M,
work Cable Pattern, sl M, k1, p1, sl 1, k2tog, psso, rib to end - 39 sts.

Rnds 15-18: Rib as set to first M, sl M, work Cable Pattern to next M, sl M, rib to end.

Rnd 19: [K1, p1] 5 times, sl 1, k2tog, psso, p1, k1, sl M,
work Cable Pattern, sl M, k1, p1, sl 1, k2tog, psso, rib to end - 35 sts.

Rnds 20-23: As Rnd 15.

Rnd 24: [K1, p1] 4 times, sl 1, k2tog, psso, p1, k1, sl M,
work Cable Pattern, sl M, k1, p1,
sl 1, k2tog, psso, rib to end - 31 sts.

Rnds 25-29: As Rnd 15.

Note: The new M's placed on next rnd should be of a different color to indicate Thumb Gusset.**

To Shape Thumb Gusset:

Rnd 30: Rib as set to first M, sl M, work Cable Pattern, sl M, k1, p1, place M, inc one st in next st knitwise, p1, inc one st in next st knitwise, place a M, rib to end - 5 sts between new M's for Thumb Gusset.

Rnd 31: Rib to first M, sl M, work Cable Pattern, sl M, k1, p1, sl M, k to next M, sl M, rib to end.

Rnd 32: Rib as set to first M, sl M, work Cable Pattern, sl M, k1, p1, sl M, inc one st in next st knitwise, k3, inc one st in next st knitwise, sl M, rib to end - 7 sts between new M's for Thumb Gusset.

Rnd 33: As Rnd 31.

Rnd 34: Rib as set to first M, sl M, work Cable Pattern, sl M, k1, p1, sl M, inc one st in next st knitwise, k5, inc one st in next st knitwise, sl M, rib to end - 9 sts between new M's for Thumb Gusset.

Rnd 35: As Rnd 31.

Rnd 36: Rib as set to first M, sl M, work Cable Pattern, sl M, k1, p1, sl M, inc one st in next st knitwise, k7, inc one st in next st knitwise, sl M, rib to end - 11 sts between new M's for Thumb Gusset.

Rnds 37 and 38: As Rnd 31.

Rnd 39: Rib as set to first M, sl M, work Cable Pattern, sl M, k1, p1, remove next M, slip next 11 sts onto a scrap piece for thumb, remove M, cast on 3 sts, rib to end - 31 sts.

Next Rnd: Rib as set to first M, sl M, work Cable Pattern, sl M, rib to end. Repeat this last rnd until mitten measures to desired length, allowing 1.5" [4 cm] for shaping top.

#To Shape Tip of Mitten:

Next Rnd: Rib as set to 3 sts before first M, sl 1, k2tog, psso, sl M, p1, k2tog, [p1, k1] 3 times, p1, sl M, sl 1, k2tog, psso, rib to end - 27 sts.

Next Rnd: Work in ribbing as set, slipping M's.

Next Rnd: Rib as set to 3 sts before first M, sl 1, k2tog, psso, sl M, p1, [k1, p1] 4 times, sl M, sl 1, k2tog, psso, rib to end - 23 sts.

Next Rnd: Work in ribbing as set, slipping M's.

Next Rnd: K1, *k2tog; rep from * to end - 12 sts.
Cut yarn, leaving a long tail.
Thread tail through rem sts, draw up tightly and fasten off securely.

Thumb: With right side of Mitten facing, starting at cast on sts of Rnd 39, pick up and k2 sts, now working sts from Thumb Gusset, using 2nd needle, k5, using 3rd needle, k6 - 13 sts.

Next Rnd: K to last 2 sts, k2tog - 12 sts. Now continue in St st (every rnd k) until Thumb measures 2" [5 cm] or desired length, from pick up row.

Next Rnd: [K2tog] 6 times - 6 sts.
Cut yarn, leaving a tail.
Thread tail through rem sts, draw up tightly and fasten off securely.
Weave in all ends.#

Left Mitten: Work as for Right Mitten from ** to **.

To Shape Thumb Gusset:

Rnd 30: Rib as set to 5 sts before first M, place a marker, inc one st in next st knitwise, p1, inc one st in next st knitwise, place a M, p1, k1, sl M, work Cable Pattern, sl M, rib to end - 5 sts between new M's for Thumb Gusset.

Rnd 31: Rib to first M, sl M, k to next M, sl M, p1, k1, sl M, work Cable Pattern, sl M, rib to end.

Rnd 32: Rib as set to first M, sl M, inc one st in next st knitwise, k3, inc one st in next st knitwise, sl M, p1, k1, sl M, work Cable Pattern, sl M, rib to end - 7 sts between new M's for Thumb Gusset.

Rnd 33: As Rnd 31.

Rnd 34: Rib as set to first M, sl M, inc one st in next st knitwise, k5, inc one st in next st knitwise, sl M, p1, k1, sl M, work Cable Pattern, sl M, rib to end - 9 sts between new M's for Thumb Gusset.

Rnd 35: As Rnd 31.

Rnd 36: Rib as set to first M, sl M, inc one st in next st knitwise, k7, inc one st in next st knitwise, sl M, p1, k1, sl M, work Cable Pattern, sl M, rib to end - 11 sts between new M's for Thumb Gusset.

Rnds 37 and 38: As Rnd 31.

Rnd 39: Rib as set to first M, remove M, slip next 11 sts onto a scrap piece for thumb, cast on 3 sts, remove M, p1, k1, sl M, work Cable Pattern, sl M, rib to end - 31 sts.

Next Rnd: Rib as set to first M, sl M, work Cable Pattern, sl M, rib to end. Repeat this last rnd until mitten measures to desired length, allowing 1.5" [4 cm] for shaping top.

Repeat from # to # as given for Right Mitten.

HAT

Cast on 66 sts, having 22 sts on each of 3 needles.

Join in rnd, taking care that sts are not twisted.

Now work in k1, p1 ribbing for 6" [15 cm].

To Shape Crown:

Rnd 1: *Sl 1, k2tog, psso, p1, k1, p1; rep from * around - 44 sts.

Rnds 2-5: *K1, p1; rep from * around.

Rnd 6: *Sl 1, k2tog, psso, p1; rep from * around - 22 sts.

Rnd 7: As Rnd 2.

Rnd 8: [Ssk] 11 times - 11 sts.

Cut yarn, leaving a long tail. Thread tail through rem sts, draw up tightly to close and fasten off securely.

Cabled Band:

Using 2 needles and working back and forth, cast on 4 sts.

Row 1: (right side) Knit.

Row 2: Inc one st purlwise in each st across - 8 sts.

Now work in Cable Pattern as follows:

Row 1: Knit.

Row 2: Purl.

Row 3: P1, T3B, T3F, p1.

Row 4: K1, p2, k2, p2, k1.

Row 5: T3B, p2, T3F.

Row 6: P2, k4, p2.

Repeat these 6 rows of pattern until band measures about 24" [61 cm] or length required to fit comfortably around head (overlapping 1" [2.5 cm]), ending after a Row 6. Cast off knitwise.

Sew a button to center of last rep of Cable worked.

Use the hole created when Row 1 of the second pattern repeat was worked as the buttonhole.

To Complete:

Place Hat on a Head (to keep fabric stretched), then with right side of Cabled Band facing, position around base of Hat about 1" [2.5 cm] above cast on edge.

Button ends together.

Sew band in place as desired.

Hat and Boot Cuff Set

Shown on page 15.

■■■□ INTERMEDIATE

SHOPPING LIST

Yarn (Worsted Weight) MEDIUM 4

Mary Maxim Starlette Ragg
[3.5 oz, 191 yards
(100 grams, 175 meters) per ball]:

☐ Black Ragg   3 balls

Knitting Needles

Set of 5 Double Point Needles

☐ Size 8 (5.00 mm)

or size needed for gauge

Additional Supplies

☐ Markers

SIZE INFORMATION

Hat: 19" [48 cm] circumference
Cuffs: 11" [28 cm] diameter x 9"
[23 cm] long

GAUGE INFORMATION

Cable (12 sts) = 2.25" [5.5 cm] wide
and 12 rows to 2" [5 cm] measured
over pattern, using **suggested**
needles or any size needles which will
give the correct gauge.

STITCH GUIDE

C6B   Slip next 3 sts onto cable
needle and hold to back of work,
k3 from left needle, then k3 from
cable needle.

C6F   Slip next 3 sts onto cable
needle and hold to front of work,
k3 from left needle, then k3 from
cable needle.

INSTRUCTIONS

BOOT CUFFS

Cast on 64 sts and divide evenly onto
4 needles (16 sts each needle).
Join in rnd, being careful that sts are
not twisted.
Place a marker on last st to indicate
end of rnds.

Ribbing:

Rnd 1: *K2, p2; rep from * around.
Repeat Rnd 1 until cuff measures
4" [10 cm] from cast on edge.
Now work in Cable pattern as follows:
Rnd 1: [K 12, p4] 4 times.
Rnds 2-4: As Rnd 1.
Rnd 5: [C6B, C6F, p4] 4 times.
Rnds 6-10: As Rnd 1.
Repeat these 10 rnds once more.
Next Rnd: *P2, k2; rep from * around.
Repeat this last rnd 7 times more.
Cast off in rib.
Weave in all ends.

Repeat for 2nd Cuff.

Wear Boot Cuffs with ribbed section in
top of boot or wear Boot Cuffs outside
boots and have ribbing turned down
or left full length!

13

HAT

Cast on 88 sts and divide evenly onto 4 needles (22 sts each needle).

Join in rnd, being careful that sts are not twisted.

Place a marker on last st to indicate end of rnds.

Work in k2, p2 ribbing for 3" [7.5 cm].

Next 3 Rnds: *P2, k2; rep from * around.

Next 3 Rnds: *K2, p2; rep from * around.

Next 3 Rnds: *P2, k2; rep from * around.

Next Rnd: Knit, inc 12 sts evenly around. (100 sts)

Now work in k2, p2 ribbing for 6" [15 cm].

Next Rnd: *K2tog, p2; rep from * around. (75 sts)

Next Rnd: *K1, p2; rep from * around.

Next Rnd: *K1, p2tog; rep from * around. (50 sts)

Next Rnd: *K1, p1; rep from * around.

Next Rnd: *K2tog; rep from * around. (25 sts)

Next Rnd: Knit.

Next Rnd: K1, [k2tog] 12 times. (13 sts)

Cut yarn, leaving a long tail.

Thread tail through rem sts and draw up tightly. Fasten off securely.

POMPOM

Cut a 5" [12.5 cm] length of yarn and set aside for the moment.

Wrap yarn around 3 fingers about 100 times.

Remove middle finger carefully, then wrap the cut length of yarn around center tightly and tie off securely, leaving tails for sewing.

Cut loops at each end.

Trim ends to form a nice round pompom as desired.

Using tails, sew pompom securely to top of Hat.

Highlander Wrap

■■■▢ INTERMEDIATE

SHOPPING LIST

Yarn (Worsted Weight)

Mary Maxim Woodlands

[3.5 ounces, 200 yards
(100 grams, 184 meters) per ball]:

☐ Charcoal   3 balls
☐ Cranberry   1 ball
☐ Green   1 ball

Knitting Needles

☐ Size 10 (6 mm)

or size needed for gauge

Additional Supplies

☐ Markers

SIZE INFORMATION

Finished: 16" x 50" [40.5 x 127 cm]

GAUGE INFORMATION

16 sts and 30 rows to 4" [10 cm], measured over Garter stitch using **suggested** needles or any size needles which will give the correct stitch gauge.

— STITCH GUIDE —

kfb   knit into front and back of next st

Note: Remember always to cross yarns when changing colors to avoid leaving a hole in the knitting. Wrap is worked from side to side.

INSTRUCTIONS

Using Green, cast on 6 sts.

Rows 1 and 2: Knit.

Row 3: Using Cranberry, k into 1st st, but do not drop from left needle, using Green, k again into same st and slip from needle, then k rem 5 sts.

Row 4: Using Green, k6, using Cranberry, k1.

Row 5: (right side) Using Cranberry, kfb, using Green, k6.

Row 6: Using Green, k6, using Cranberry, k2.

Row 7: Using Cranberry k1, kfb, using Green, k6.

Row 8 and following alternate rows: Keeping colors correct, knit.

Row 9: Using Cranberry, k2, kfb, using Green, k6.

Row 11: Using Charcoal, k into 1st st, but do not drop from left needle, using Cranberry, k again into same st and sl from needle, k3, using Green, k6.

Row 13: Using Charcoal, kfb, using Cranberry, k4, using Green, k6.

Row 15: Using Charcoal, k1, kfb, place a marker, using Cranberry, k4, using Green, k6.

Row 17: Using Charcoal, k2, kfb, sl marker (M), using Cranberry, k4, using Green, k6.

Row 19: Using Charcoal, k3, kfb, sl M, using Cranberry, k4, using Green, k6.

Row 21: Using Charcoal, k3, kfb, k to M, sl M, using Cranberry, k4, using Green, k6.

Row 22: Keeping colors correct, knit.

Repeat these last 2 rows until there are 64 sts on the needle, ending after a Row 22.

Place a marker at end of last row (to work for measurement later).

Next Row: As Row 21.

Keeping colors correct, k 3 rows. Repeat last 4 rows until piece measures 5" [12.5 cm] from last M placed, ending after a Row 4.

Next Row: *(dec row)* Keeping colors correct, k3, sl 1, k1, psso, k to end. Knit 3 rows.

Repeat last 4 rows until piece measures 10" [25.5 cm] from last M placed, ending after a Row 4.

Now continue to dec as follows, keeping colors correct as set:

Row 1: K3, sl 1, k1, psso, k to end.

Row 2: Knit to end.

Repeat these last 2 rows until 14 sts rem, ending after a Row 2.

Next Row: K1, sl 1, k1, psso, k to end.

Next Row: Knit.

Repeat last 2 rows once more.

Next Row: Sl 1, k1, psso, k to end.

Next Row: Using Green, k6, using Cranberry, k4.

Next Row: Using Cranberry, k2tog, k2, using Green, k6.

Next Row: Knit, using colors as set.

Next Row: Using Cranberry, k1, sl 1, k1, psso, using Green, k6.

Next Row: Knit, using colors as set.

Repeat last 2 rows once more.

Next Row: Sl 1, k1, psso, k to end. (7 sts)

Next Row: Knit.

Next Row: Using Green, k2tog, k to end.

Cast off knitwise.

Weave in all ends.

Grooved Cowl

 EASY

SHOPPING LIST

Yarn (Light Worsted)

Mary Maxim Milan

[3.5 ounces, 219 yards
(100 grams, 200 meters) per ball]:

☐ Sicily   3 balls

Knitting Needle

24" [60 cm] Circular Needle

☐ Size 8 (5.00 mm)

or size needed for gauge

Additional Supplies

☐ Marker

SIZE INFORMATION

Finished: 15" x 38" [38 x 96.5 cm]

GAUGE INFORMATION

9 sts and 24 rows to 2" [2.5 cm] over pattern, without stretching, using **suggested needle** or any size needle which will give the correct gauge.

INSTRUCTIONS

Cast on 190 sts loosely.

Join in rnd, taking care not to twist sts and place a marker after last st to indicate start of rnds.

Slip marker on each rnd.

Now work in pattern as follows:

Rnds 1-6: Knit.

Rnds 7-12: Purl.

Repeat these 12 rnds until work measures 15" [38 cm] from cast on edge (without any stretching), ending after a Row 6 or Row 12.

Cast off purlwise. Weave in ends.

Wear as a long infinity scarf or wrap around neck and wear as a cozy cowl.

Quick Knit Wrap

▮▮▮▮▯ **INTERMEDIATE**

SHOPPING LIST

Yarn (Super Bulky)

Mary Maxim Quick

[7 ounces, 87 yards
(200 grams, 80 meters) per ball]:

Size Small/Medium

☐ Any Color   5 balls

Size Large/XLarge

☐ Any Color   6 balls

Knitting Needle

32" (80 cm) Circular Needle

☐ Size 17 (12.0 mm)

or size needed for gauge

Additional Supplies

☐ 1.5" (38 mm) Button
☐ Sewing needle
☐ Matching thread

SIZE INFORMATION

Bottom Circumference:
90(95)" [228.5(241.5) cm]

Length from Back Neck:
17.5 (20)" [44.5 (51) cm]

GAUGE INFORMATION

8 sts to 4" [10 cm] and 16 rows to 5" [12.5 cm] using **suggested** needle or any size needle which will give the correct gauge.

— STITCH GUIDE —

W&T Bring yarn to front of work, slip next st to right-hand needle, take yarn to back of work, then move slipped st back to left-hand needle, bring yarn back to front of work and turn work.

INSTRUCTIONS

Starting at front edge of Left Front, cast on 35(40) sts.

Knit 4 rows (counts as front band). Now working lengthwise around to front edge of Right Front, work in short row pattern as follows:

**Row 1: (mark as right side) K5, W&T.
Row 2 and every alternate row: Knit to end.
Row 3: K 10, W&T.
Row 5: K 15, W&T.
Row 7: K 20, W&T.
Row 9: K 25, W&T.
Row 11: K 30, W&T.
Row 12: As Row 2.

Size Lge/Xlge Only
Next Row: K 35, W&T.
Next Row: As Row 2.

All Sizes:
Next Row: K 35(40).
Next Row: Sl 1, k to end.#
Next Row: K 35(40).

Next Row: Sl 1, p to end.**

Now rep from ** to ** 15(16) times more, then rep from ** to # once.

Next Row: Buttonhole Row: Knit to last 5 sts, k2tog, [yo] twice, k3.

Next Row: K3, k into first yo and drop 2nd yo from needle, k to end - 35(40) sts.

Knit 3 rows. Cast off knitwise.

These last 4 rows count as front band.

Collar: With right side of wrap facing, pick up and k 33(37) sts evenly spaced around neck edge.

Row 1: (wrong side) P2, *k1, p1; rep from * to last st, p1.

Row 2: K2, *p1, k1; rep from * to last st, k1.

Repeat these 2 rows twice more.

Next Row: (inc row) P2, *inc one st in next st knitwise, p1; rep from * to last 3 sts, inc one st in next st knitwise, p2 - 48(54) sts.

Next Row: K2, *p2, k1; rep from * to last st, k1.

Next Row: P2, *k2, p1; rep from * to last st, p1.

Repeat these last 2 rows 3 times more.

Cast off in pattern.

To Complete:

Sew a button securely on Left Front band, opposite buttonhole.

Weave in all ends, taking care with those on Collar as it folds back to outside.

Claire's Fingerless Gloves

■■■▢ INTERMEDIATE

SIZE INFORMATION

Size: 8" [20.5 cm] long x 9" [23 cm]
circumference (above thumb)

GAUGE INFORMATION

Cabled Band = 4.5" [11.5 cm] wide,
using **suggested** needles or any size
needles which will give the correct
stitch gauge.

— STITCH GUIDE —

DPN's   Double point needles

C2B   Slip next st onto cable
needle and hold to back of work,
k1 from left needle, then k1 from
cable needle.

C4F   Slip next 2 sts onto cable
needle and hold to front of work,
k2 from left needle, then k2 sts from
cable needle.

C4B   Slip next 2 sts onto cable
needle and hold to back of work,
k2 from left needle, then k2 sts from
cable needle.

T4F   Slip next 2 sts onto cable
needle and hold to front of work,
p2 from left needle, k2 sts from cable
needle.

T4B   Slip next 2 sts onto cable
needle and hold to back of work,
k2 from left needle, then p2 sts from
cable needle.

T5F   Slip next 2 sts onto cable
needle and hold to front of work,
p3 from left needle, k2 sts from cable
needle.

T5B   Slip next 3 sts onto cable
needle and hold to back of work,
k2 from left needle, then p3 sts from
cable needle.

C4BDEC   Slip next 2 sts to cable
needle and hold to back of work,
[insert needle through next st on
left-hand needle and first st on cable
needle and k2tog] twice.

C4FDEC   Slip next 2 sts to cable
needle and hold to front of work,
[insert needle through first st on
cable needle and next st on left-hand
needle and k2tog] twice.

W&T   Bring yarn to front of work,
slip next st to right-hand needle,
take yarn to back of work, then move
slipped st back to left-hand needle,
bring yarn back to front of work and
turn work.

Note: Cabled band that wraps around
hand is worked in a straight band
that is sewn together at thumb side.
Ribbing sts are picked up when that is
done and worked in the round.

INSTRUCTIONS

Cabled Band:

Using 2 DPN's, cast on 28 sts.

Beginning Rows 1 and 2: Knit.

Beginning Row 3: (inc row) K3, p2, C2B, p2, [inc one st in next st knitwise] twice, p6, [inc one st in next st knitwise] twice, p2, C2B, p2, k3. (32 sts)

Now work in pattern as follows:

Row 1: (wrong side) P3, k2, p2, k2, p4, k6, p4, k2, p2, k2, p3.

Row 2: K3, p2, C2B, p2, C4F, p6, C4B, p2, C2B, p2, k3.

Row 3: As Row 1.

Row 4: K3, p2, C2B, p2, k2, T4F, p2, T4B, k2, p2, C2B, p2, k3.

Row 5: P3, [k2, p2] 6 times, k2, p3.

Row 6: K3, p2, C2B, p2, T4F, k2, p2, k2, T4B, p2, C2B, p2, k3.

Row 7: P3, k2, p2, k4, p4, k2, p4, k4, p2, k2, p3.

Row 8: K3, p2, C2B, p4, T5F, T5B, p4, C2B, p2, k3.

Row 9: P3, k2, p2, k7, p4, k7, p2, k2, p3.

Row 10: K3, p2, C2B, p7, C4F, p7, C2B, p2, k3.

Row 11: Work as Row 9.

Row 12: K3, p2, C2B, p4, T5B, T5F, p4, C2B, p2, k3.

Row 13: Work as Row 7.

Row 14: K3, p2, C2B, p2, T4B, k2, p2, k2, T4F, p2, C2B, p2, k3.

Row 15: Work as Row 5.

Row 16: K3, p2, C2B, p2, k2, T4B, p2, T4F, k2, p2, C2B, p2, k3.

Repeat Rows 1-16 twice more, then Row 1 once.

Next Row: K3, p2, C2B, p2, C4FDEC, p6, C4BDEC, p2, C2B, p2, k3. (28 sts)

Knit 2 rows.

Next Row: Cast off 12 sts, k to end. (16 sts)

Next Row: Knit.

Thumb Gusset:

Row 1: K4, W&T, k4.

Row 2: K8, W&T, k8.

Row 3: K 12, W&T, k 12.

Rows 4 and 5: K 16.

Repeat Rows 1-5 once more.

Cast off knitwise.

Bring cast on and cast off edges of Cabled Band together.

Sew cast off edge of Thumb Gussett to cast on edge, then sew remainder of seam above thumb opening.

Ribbing:

Using DPN's, with right side of Cabled Band facing and working around bottom edge, pick up and k 44 sts evenly around, dividing sts onto 3 needles. (14:16:14)

Place a marker on last st to indicate end of rnds.

Work in k2, p2 ribbing for 2.5" [6 cm].

Next Rnd: *K2, p1, inc one st in next st purlwise; rep from * around. (55 sts)

Next Rnd: *K2, p3; rep from * around.

Repeat last rnd until ribbing measures 3.5" [9 cm] from beg.

Cast off in pattern.

Weave in all ends.

Repeat to make second glove.

Broken Rib Scarf

 EASY

SIZE INFORMATION

Finished: 11" x 44" [28 x 111.5 cm]

GAUGE INFORMATION

7 sts and 8 rows to 4" [10 cm],
measured over pattern using
2 strands of yarn and **suggested**
needles or any size needles which
will give the correct stitch gauge.

INSTRUCTIONS

Using 2 strands of yarn throughout,
cast on 19 sts.

Now work in Broken rib as follows:

Row 1: K1, *p1, k1; rep from * to end.

Row 2: Knit.

Repeat these 2 rows for pattern, until piece measures 44" [111.5 cm] from beg. Cast off ribwise.

Weave in all ends.

Optional: Sew a button to one side of scarf at desired point.

Push button through sts of opposite end to wear as a wrap.

Claire's Cowl

 EASY

SIZE INFORMATION

Finished: 8" x 42" [20.5 x 106.5 cm]

GAUGE INFORMATION

7.5 sts and 8 rows to 4" [10 cm],
measured over Garter st using
suggested needles or any size
needles which will give the correct
gauge.

INSTRUCTIONS

Using 2 strands of yarn throughout,
cast on 15 sts. Work in Garter st (every
row knit), until piece measures 42"
[106.5 cm] from cast on edge, or to
desired length. Cast off knitwise.

To Complete: Lay piece out flat.
Turn one end once, then bring the
cast on and cast off edges together,
side by side. Sew edges together.

Wear cowl loose to cover shoulders or
wrap around neck once to give extra
warmth.

Quick Cowl

SHOPPING LIST

Yarn (Super Bulky)

Mary Maxim Quick

[7 ounces, 87 yards
(200 grams, 80 meters) per ball]:

☐ Any Color   2 balls

Knitting Needle

24" (60 cm) Circular Needle

☐ Size 17 (12.0 mm)

or size needed for gauge

Additional Supplies

☐ Marker

SIZE INFORMATION

Finished: 7" x 32" [18 x 81 cm]

GAUGE INFORMATION

8 sts and 14 rows to 4" [10 cm],
measured over pattern using
suggested needle or any size needle
which will give the correct stitch
gauge.

INSTRUCTIONS

Cast on 64 sts and join in rnd, taking
care that sts are not twisted. Place
a marker after last st to indicate
beginning of rnds.

Rnd 1: Knit.

Rnds 2-4: *K3, p5; rep from * around.

Rnd 5: Knit.

Rnds 6-8: *P4, k3, p1; rep from *
around.

Repeat these 8 rnds once more, then
Rnds 1-4 once.

Cast off knitwise. Weave in all ends.

General Instructions

ABBREVIATIONS

"	inches		mm	milimeter	
approx.	approximately		rem	remain or remaining	
beg	begin or beginning		rep	repeat	
CC	Contrast Color		rnd	round	
cm	centimeter		sl	slip	
dec	decrease or decreasing		st	stitch	
inc	increase or increasing		sts	stitches	
k	knit		St st	Stocking stitch	
p	purl		tog	together	
psso	pass slipped stitch over		yds	yards	
M	marker		yo	yarn over	
MC	Main Color				

SYMBOLS & TERMS

* or # work instructions following or between * or # as many more times as indicated in addition to the first time.

() or [ ] work enclosed instructions as many times as specified by the number immediately following **or** work all enclosed instructions in the stitch or space indicated **or** contains explanatory remarks

— the number(s) given after a hyphen at the end of a row or round denote(s) the number of stitches or spaces you should have on that row or round.

KNIT TERMINOLOGY

UNITED STATES		INTERNATIONAL
gauge	=	tension
bind off	=	cast off

Yarn Weight Symbol & Names	1 SUPER FINE	2 FINE	3 LIGHT	4 MEDIUM	5 BULKY	6 SUPER BULKY	7 JUMBO
Type of Yarns in Category	Sock, Fingering Baby	Sport, Baby	DK, Light Worsted	Worsted, Afghan Aran	Chunky, Craft, Rug	Super Bulky, Roving	Jumbo, Roving
Knit Gauge Range in Stockinette St to 4" (10 cm)	27-32 sts	23-26 sts	21-24 sts	16-20 sts	12-15 sts	7-11 sts	6 sts and fewer
Advised Needle Size Range	1 to 3	3 to 5	5 to 7	7 to 9	9 to 11	11 to 17	17 and larger

*GUIDELINES ONLY: The chart above reflects the most commonly used gauges and needle sizes for specific yarn categories.

BEGINNER	Projects for first-time knitters using basic knit and purl stitches. Minimal shaping.
EASY	Projects using basic stitches, repetitve stitch patterns, simple color changes, and simple shaping and finishing.
INTERMEDIATE	Projects with a variety of stitches, such as basic cables and lace, simple intarsia, double-pointed needles and knitting in the round needle techniques, mid-level shaping and finishing.
EXPERIENCED	Projects using advanced techniques and stitches, such as short rows, fair isle, more intricate intarsia, cables, lace patterns and numerous color changes.

KNITTING NEEDLES

U.S.	50	35	19	17	15	13	11	----	----	10.5	10	9	8	7	6	5	4	3	----	2	1	0	----
U.K.	---	----	----	----	000	00	0	1	2	3	4	5	6	7	8	9	----	10	11	12	13	14	15
Metric mm	25	19	15	12.75	10	9	8	7.5	7	6.5	6	5.5	5	4.5	4	3.75	3.5	3.25	3	2.75	2.25	2	1.75

Casting On

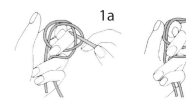

1a. Make a slip knot: Loop the yarn as shown and slip needle under the lower strand of the loop.
1b. Pull up a loop of yarn.

2. Pull the yarn end attached to the ball of yarn to tighten the slip knot leaving the other end approx. 4" [10 cm] long. Transfer needle to left hand.

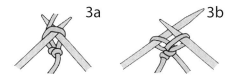

3a. Insert the right-hand needle through slip knot and wind yarn over right-hand needle.
3b. Pull loop through slip knot.

4. Place new loop on left-handle needle. (You now have 2 stitches (sts) on your left-hand needle.)

5. Insert right-hand needle between last 2 stitches (sts) on left-hand needle and wind yarn over right-hand needle.

6. Pull loop through. Place this new loop on left-hand needle beside last stitch (st). (You now have 1 more stitch on left-hand needle). Repeat (rep) steps 5 and 6 until required number of stitches (sts) have been cast on left-hand needle.

The Knit Stitch

1. Hold the needle with cast on stitches (sts) in your left hand, and the loose yarn attached to the ball at the back of work. Insert right-hand needle from left to right through the front of the first stitch (st) on the left-hand needle.

2. Wind the yarn from left to right over the point of the right-hand needle.

3. Draw the yarn through this original stitch (st) which forms a new stitch (st) on right-hand needle.

 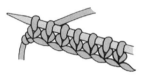

4. Slip the original stitch (st) off the left-hand needle, keeping the new stitch (st) on the right-hand needle.

5. To knit a row, repeat steps 1 to 4 until all stitches (sts) have been transferred from left-hand needle to right-hand needle. Turn the work by transferring the needle with stitches (sts) into your left hand to knit the next row.

The Purl Stitch

1. With yarn at front of work, insert right-hand needle from right to left through front of first stitch (st) on left-hand needle.

2. Wind yarn around right-hand needle. Pull yarn through stitch (st).

3. Slip original stitch (st) off needle. Repeat (rep) these steps until all stitches (sts) on left-hand needle have been transferred onto right-hand needle to complete one row of purling.

Increasing and Decreasing

 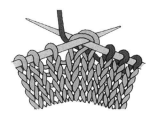 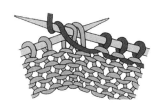

Increase 1 stitch (st) in next stitch (st): Work into front and back of stitch (st) as follows: Knit stitch (st), then before slipping it off needle, twist right-hand needle behind left-hand needle and knit again into back of loop. Slip original stitch (st) off needle. There are now 2 stitches (sts) on right-hand needle made from original stitch.

K2tog Decrease: Knit 2 stitches (sts) together (tog) through the front of both loops.

P2tog Decrease: Purl 2 stitches (sts) together (tog) through the front of both loops.

Casting Off

Cast off using knit stitch (knitwise): Knit the first 2 stitches (sts). *Using left-hand needle, lift first stitch (st) over second stitch (st) and drop it off between points of the 2 needles. Knit the next stitch (st); repeat (rep) from * until all stitches (sts) from left-hand needle have been worked and only 1 stitch (st) remains on the right-hand needle. Cut yarn (leaving enough to sew in end) and thread cut end through stitch (st) on needle. Draw yarn up firmly to fasten off last stitch (st).

Cast off using purl stitch (purlwise): Purl first 2 stitches (sts). *Using left-hand needle, lift first stitch (st) over second stitch (st) and drop it off needle. Purl next stitch (st) as described for casting off knitwise.

Yarn Information

Projects in this book were made with different weight yarns. Any brand of yarn may be used.
It is best to refer to yardage/meters when determining how many balls or skeins to purchase.
Remember, to arrive at the finished size, it is the GAUGE/TENSION that is important, not the brand of yarn.
For your convenience, listed below are the specific yarn ranges used to create our photographed models.

Ribbed Cowl
Mary Maxim's Quick

Grooved Cowl
Mary Maxim's Milan

Cable & Rib Scarf
Mary Maxim's Milan

Quick Knit Wrap
Mary Maxim's Quick

Classic Tam
Mary Maxim's Classic

Claire's Fingerless Gloves
Mary Maxim's Woodlands

Arrowhead Cable Set
Mary Maxim's Titan

Broken Rib Scarf
Mary Maxim's Titan

Hat and Boot Cuff Set
Mary Maxim's Starlette Ragg

Claire's Cowl
Mary Maxim's Titan

Highlander Wrap
Mary Maxim's Woodlands

Quick Cowl
Mary Maxim's Quick